What Rot!
Nature's Mighty Recycler

By Elizabeth Ring

Photographs by Dwight Kuhn

The Millbrook Press
Brookfield, Connecticut

For Homer, everlasting
E.R.

For Ashley
D.K.

Library of Congress Cataloging-in-Publication Data
Ring, Elizabeth 1920–
What rot! : nature's mighty recycler / text by Elizabeth Ring;
photos by Dwight Kuhn.
p. cm.
Summary: Text and photos show how rot and all the tiny
organisms that cause it maintain the cycle of life.
ISBN 1-56294-671-4 (lib. bdg.)
1. Biodegradation—Juvenile literature. 2. Death (Biology)—
Juvenile literature. [1. Biodegradation. 2. Ecology.] I. Kuhn,
Dwight, ill. II. Title.
QH530.5.R56   1996   95-353   574.2—dc20   CIP   AC

What Rot!

. . . into brittle brown lace. In the end, the leaves crumble away. That's okay, though. That's just nature keeping the cycle of life rolling by making things change all the time.

Without rot, leaves and other dead things would pile up, miles high. They could smother the earth. New plants couldn't grow. The truth is that without rot the whole world could die.

Rot is a mighty force that never stops moving. It slowly decays whatever is dying or dead. It weakens the strongest tree you might climb.

What causes rot? Rotters are mostly animals and plants: mammals, insects, birds, and especially *microbes*. To live, they all need food and shelter—and they find plenty of both in a dying or dead tree.

One day, at a pumpkin patch, you pick a plump pumpkin. You carve a face in its head—your Jack-o'-lantern for Halloween. You'd like its wide, friendly smile to last forever and ever.

But soon, the pumpkin sags. Now it wears a weird grin.

Before long, spots of *mold* pop out on the pumpkin's soft head—like blue chicken pox. Your pumpkin's got a bad case of pumpkin rot.

Rot sometimes seems really rotten. It can ruin things you may like a lot—like pumpkins or apples or flowers.

Rot makes a crisp, juicy apple shrivel up and turn brown. It dusts the skin of the apple with white, fuzzy mold.

Rot makes a bright-
petaled daffodil. . .

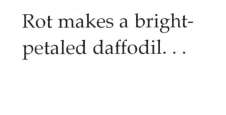

. . . droop its head
and look sad—

like a small,
burst balloon.

Rot changes splashy fall leaves . . .

Dozens of different kinds of rotters invade a tree as it dies. Some of these rotters, like *bacteria*, are microbes that are too small to see—except under a microscope. Other microbes, called *fungi*, also feed on the tree. You can sometimes see fungi fruits, such as mushrooms, when they push out from the tree's bark. Millions of microbes live inside the tree—feeding, growing, spreading, dying, and, all the while, breaking down the tree's wood.

Many kinds of *beetles* crawl on the tree. Some kinds poke into cracks in the bark, hunting for insects swarming inside the tree. When this click beetle, which eats very little, was a young wireworm (a *larva*), it lived both in the ground and under the tree's bark.

Other insects poke, scratch, and chew. Small cracks in the bark become holes. Rain, ice, snow, and dew seep under the bark. There, in the dark, microbes thrive and spread. The wood gets softer each day. Woodpeckers and other birds chip away, hunting insects, making nests.

An owl makes its home in a hollow where two branches meet.

A chipmunk digs a burrow at the tree's loosening roots.

All this rotting activity weakens the tree, hour upon hour. Rot reaches into the tree's core, and the dead tree falls to the ground. Now the tree is a log. Kick the log and you splinter the soft wood.

Termites chew at the wood and the log rots away, day after day . . . after day . . . after day.

Hundreds of *ants* live in tunnels and galleries that they scoop out of the crumbling log. Here a worker ant tends cocoons in an ant nursery.

An ichneumon wasp uses its long tail to drill through the bark and plant its eggs in tunnels other insects have made. When the eggs hatch, the wasp larvae feed on the larvae of the other insects that live in the log.

Fungi, great rotters, grow fast on a log. You sometimes see webs of fungi threads on the bark. Some are white, like a splash of spilled milk. Others look like yellow straw.

Slime mold drapes itself on the log, like a fancy lace collar.

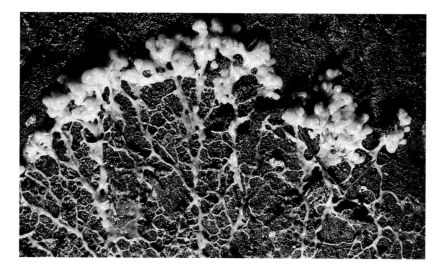

Knobs of *lichen* stand up stiff and straight, like British soldiers, which they are sometimes called. They're called Turk's caps, too. You can probably see why.

Some fungi fruits grow big and bloom in odd shapes.

Moss also is a good rotter. Moss plants cover a log like a spongy carpet and sprout little cases full of tiny seedlike grains called *spores*.

When spore cases are ripe, they explode—like small
fireworks displays. The spores are carried all over, by wind
and water, and even in or on animals that may roam far and
wide. Some spores will die, but many will settle in places
such as damp, rotting logs, where new moss plants can grow.

The day comes when a log—and every other dead thing—become part of the soil. Millions of microbes, insects, *earthworms*, snails, beetles, and other rotters in the soil continue to eat, grow, multiply, and die—all helping to enrich the soil for new growth.

Hordes of earthworms play a big role in making good soil. As they churn through the dirt, they mix bits of wood, rotten plants, bone, sand, animal droppings (including their own), and much more. The worms' tunneling also makes open spaces for air and water to circulate.

You might think the soil would smell really rotten, with all the dead stuff it holds. But no. It smells—well, earthy, almost sweet. Even before it is fully decayed, the soil feels moist and looks rich.

Every spring, when the sun warms the earth and rain soaks the ground, new life leaps straight out of the old. New green plants spring from the teeming brown soil.

As the plants grow, many animals feed on them.

When a plant dies, an earthworm may pull a leaf,
a stem, or a twig underground and eat it when it decays.

Everything eats everything else. This food chain is a big part of the cycle of life. The earthworm may be snatched by a hungry shrew.

The shrew may be caught and eaten by an owl or some other *predator*. And when that animal dies, its body, too, becomes part of the soil.

When new life grows in a forest, a field, or a garden, it always contains invisible traces of things that gave their lives to the soil. These traces hold *nutrients* that help new life grow. The cycle of life keeps turning, like a clock that will never stop.

In a way, your Halloween pumpkin is going to live on—forever. Last year's pumpkin may seem to be gone. But it's there somewhere. It gave itself to the soil—seeds and all. And the soil is giving it back in new pumpkins.

So, when you carve a smile on your pumpkin next year, you can say to yourself, "My Jack-o'-lantern die? Never! Because of what? Rot!"

More About
Rot and Rotters

Ants: Ants, like *termites*, live in huge colonies. They are strong-jawed insects that chew through wood, although they don't eat it, as termites do. They make many tunnels and "rooms" inside a rotting tree.

Bacteria: Bacteria are tiny, one-celled organisms, too small to see without a microscope. Many kinds form seedlike spores. Bacteria live everywhere, in and on everything in the world. Millions live in one pound of soil. Most bacteria can't make their own food and must live on the food made by other plants and animals or on things that are rotting.

Beetles: Beetles are insects that live underground, in water, and on plants. They have hard front wings and strong jaws. Some beetles are *scavengers*. Others are *predators* or *parasites*.

Chlorophyll: Chlorophyll is the green matter in green plants. It changes the sun's energy into chemical energy that makes it possible for plants to make the sugars they need in order to grow.

Earthworms: Earthworms live in the ground, under rocks, and in the soft wood under logs. They eat and digest rotting matter such as dead plants. Earthworms' droppings (small balls of undigested food called "castings") help make the soil rich and fertile.

Fungi: Fungi are tiny plants. Unlike green plants, which can make their own food, fungi live on food made by other plants or animals or on rotting matter. Their feeding helps break down rotting matter into soil. A fungus (one fungi) holds tight to its food source by spreading out rootlike threads, from which grow fungi fruits such as mushrooms. The fruits hold the *spores* that make new fungi. There are about 70,000 to 75,000 different kinds of fungi.

Larva: Larvae are the young of certain animals, especially insects and water creatures. They usually neither look nor behave like adults. For example, beetle larvae are wormlike grubs, and toad larvae are tadpoles.

Lichen: A lichen is a plant that is partly a colorless fungus and partly a green alga, a simple green plant. The alga nourishes the fungus with sugar, a food that a fungus needs but can't make for itself. The fungus shelters the alga and holds water in which the alga grows. Some lichens are crusty; others are shrubby or leafy. Their knobs contain fungi *spores*.

Microbes: A microbe is a plant or animal that is too small to see without using a microscope. *Bacteria* and *fungi* are microbes. Fungi are visible only when a large group of them form a mass or when their fruits—such as mushrooms—bloom.

Molds: Molds are tiny plants in the *fungi* family. Like mushrooms, molds bear *spores*. Each pin-sized mold strand on a pumpkin or apple or log holds hundreds of thousands of spores.

Moss: Moss is a small green plant that attaches itself to trees, logs, rocks, and the ground in damp, warm, shady places. Some mosses look like tiny trees or ferns, others like a thick, damp doormat. The small rootlets of moss plants break both wood and rocks into tiny pieces that become part of the soil. There are about 20,000 different kinds of mosses.

Nutrients: Substances that nourish plants and animals are called nutrients. Sugar, starch, and chemical elements (such as nitrogen) are a few of the nutrients plants and animals need.

Parasites: Parasites are plants and animals that live and feed on other plants and animals (called hosts). For example, *fungi* are plant parasites, and blood-sucking fleas are animal parasites.

Predators: Animals that hunt other animals for food are called predators. For example, owls, shrews, and weasels are predators. The animals they hunt are called their prey.

Scavengers: Scavengers are the clean-up crews of the animal world. Insects (such as beetles), birds (such as crows), and animals (such as jackals) eat up the remains of dead plants and animals.

Spores: Spores are tiny one-celled bodies, something like the seeds of green plants. Each spore case holds thousands of spores. When spores are released from their cases, they drift on wind or water (or ride in or on roaming animals) until they land on places where there is food (such as a rotting plant or animal) to grow on.

Termites: A termite is a strong-jawed, wood-eating insect. Hundreds live together in a colony. They often make their tunnels and nests in rotted trees where they and their young (called nymphs) chew the wood into bite-size pieces. Microbes that live inside termites help the termite digest the wood.

About the Author and Photographer

Freelance editor and author Elizabeth Ring has written extensively for young readers, and natural history topics have often been the focus of her work. A former teacher and an editor at *Ranger Rick*, she has written a range of programs on environmental subjects for the National Wildlife Federation. Her previous books for The Millbrook Press include two biographies, *Rachel Carson: Caring for the Earth* and *Henry David Thoreau: In Step With Nature*, as well as the Good Dogs! series, and, most recently, *Night Flier* and *Lucky Mouse*, both picture books with photographs by Dwight Kuhn. She lives in Woodbury, Connecticut.

Photographer Dwight Kuhn is well known for his studies of nature subjects, especially the beautifully composed close-ups that have appeared often in *Ranger Rick*, *World*, *National Geographic*, *Natural History*, and other magazines. Among his previous books for children are four that were named Outstanding Science Trade Books by the National Science Teachers Association and the Children's Book Council: *The Hidden Life of the Meadow*, *The Hidden Life of the Pond*, *The Hidden Life of the Forest*, and *More Than Just a Vegetable Garden*. Kuhn lives in Dexter, Maine.